Copyright (c) 2024 by Tory Envy
All rights reserved.

All rights reserved. No part of this book may be reproduced or transmitted in any form by any means, electronic or mechanical, including photocopying, recording, or by any information or retrieval systems, without the written permission of the publisher.

Paperback ISBN: 9798872589709

First Edition 2024
Edited by Yia Lee
Published by Tory Envy

My Look and Find Book
Kuv Phau Ntawv Saib Thiab Nrhiav

Written by Tory Envy

This book belongs to
Phau ntawv no yog
_____ li.

Peev Xwm is getting ready for school. Help find his things.

Peev Xwm tab tom npaj mus kawm ntawv. Pab nrhiav nws cov khoom.

It's playtime! Find toys to play with.

Txog caij mus ua si! Nrhiav khoom lo ua si.

Peev Xwm is grocery shopping. Find items to add to his cart.

Peev Xwm mus taj laj yuav zaub mov. Nrhiav khoom ntxiv rau nws lub tawb.

Peev Xwm is hungry. Find food for him to eat!

Peev Xwm tshaib plab. Nrhiav zaub mov rau nws noj.

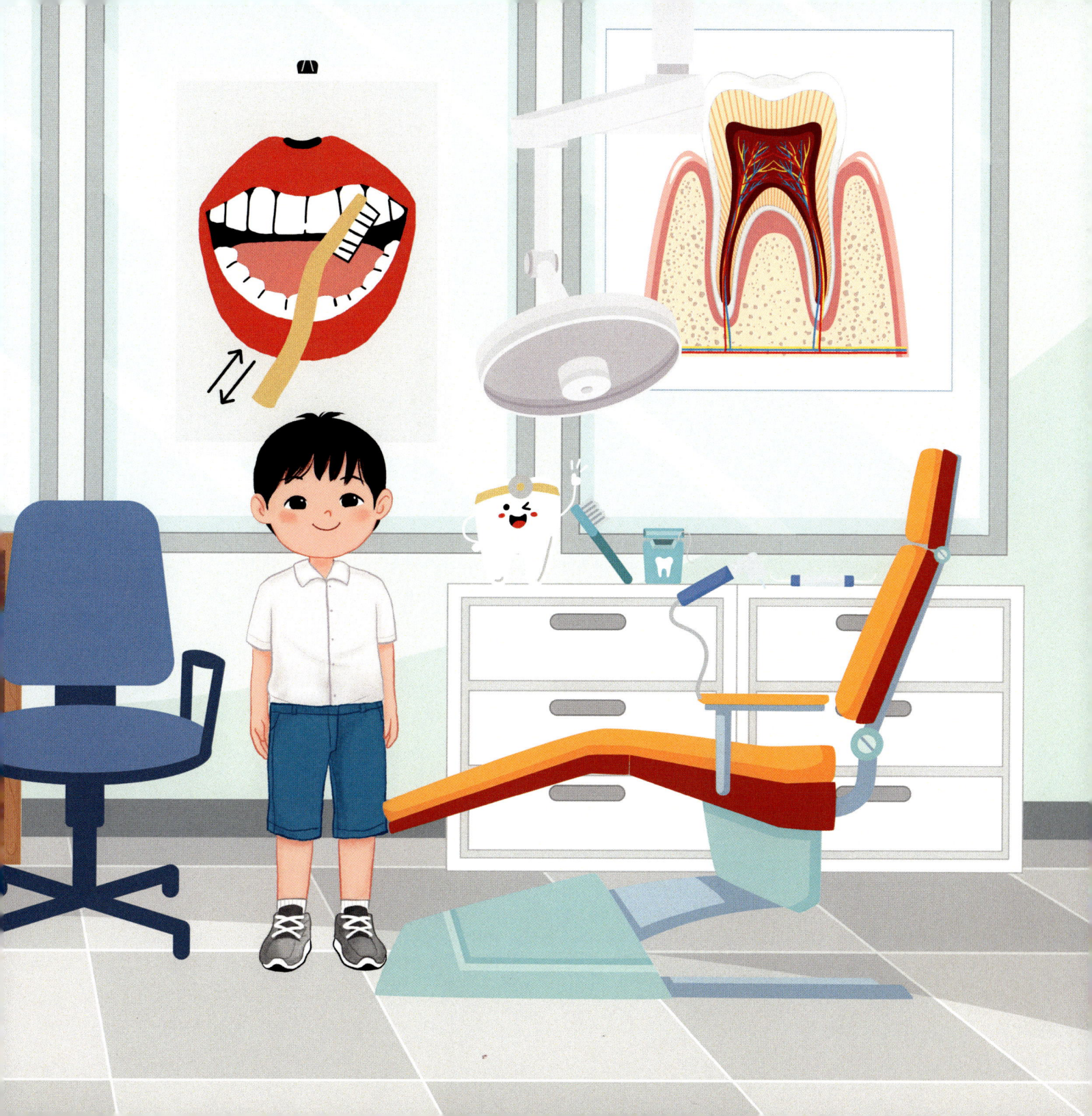

Peev Xwm is good at babysitting. Find the pictures in his living room.

Peev Xwm txawj zov me nyuam heev. Nrhiav cov duab hauv nws chav chaw nyob.

At night, Peev Xwm takes a bath. Find the items he uses to take a bath.

Thaum tsaus ntuj, Peev Xwm mus da dej. Nrhiav cov khoom siv da dej.

Victoria Lee, known professionally as Tory Envy is a Hmong-American children's book author and artist. Envy published her first Hmong and English bilingual children's book "I Am A Big Sister - Kuv Yog Ib Tug Niam Laus" in 2021 where she was featured on Fox 9 News, and ranked top 20 internationally at Amazon.com for Asian American Literature after her release.

Being the first born generation of Hmong immigrant parents in the Unites States, Envy found various forms of art as a way to express herself and share experiences from her upbringing. Being Hmong and through her books and art, she encourages self-expression and promotes diversity in children's books.

Website: toryenvy.com | @toryenvy

More books by Tory Envy.

English and Hmong Bilingual Children's book

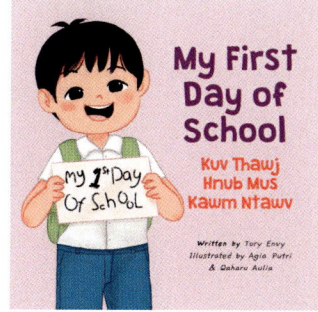

Reading books come with an interactive free YouTube video.

https://www.youtube.com/@ToryEnvy

Made in United States
Orlando, FL
27 December 2024